The Healing Power of the Goddess;
a practical approach for pagans developing in their spiritual practice and the healing arts

The Healing Power of the Goddess;

a practical approach for pagans developing in their spiritual practice and the healing arts

Pippa Lee Meer

To order additional copies of this book, contact:
Xlibris Corporation
0-800-644-6988
www.xlibrispublishing.co.uk
Orders@xlibrispublishing.co.uk
301506

CONTENTS

ACKNOWLEDGEMENTS

Many thanks to:

Jan Preston for the front cover illustration

janpreston.uk@gmail.com

Sharon Grimshaw for the back cover illustration

May all who read this book live an inspired life!

*   *   *

PREFACE

The inspiration to write this book came from an awareness that my life as a spiritual healer and Reiki master, appeared to belong in a very different 'cupboard' to that of my paganism—all be it in the same kitchen! Practically of course, this is not the case, and I realise that they sit very comfortably next to each other on the same shelf. However, I have become increasingly conscious that the healers I am working with are not pagan and the pagans I know are not all healers.

I am able to accept that the healers I work with may not choose paganism as their path; in fact it is wonderfully refreshing to note that my healer friends come from a variety of traditions, cultures and faiths, with spiritual healing as the common interest. (It is not essential to be a spiritualist to do spiritual healing.) However, I do find it perplexing that so many of my pagan friends are unfamiliar with healing, chakras, energy work and visualisation. This baffles me. And so this book is born. It is my belief regardless of tradition, that there are huge benefits to pagans learning about the healing arts, whether a wiccan, druid, shaman or hedge witch, the ability to facilitate healing is an essential string to any bow as well as for the protection and wellbeing of the practicing pagan, many of whom open up to energies they are uncertain of, putting themselves at risk. This book is a guide to developing in the healing arts safely, with practical suggestions, tips and techniques for all, as well as suggestions for developing personal spiritual practice, regularly and regardless of tradition or beliefs.

*   *   *

INTRODUCTION

There are several ways you can use this book, but one thing I would recommend is that you keep a notebook. You might choose to call it a journal. It's essentially an opportunity to record your personal growth and spiritual practice and by dating the entries you will be able to review how much you have learned and developed, or if something significant has occurred. It might be a dream or some synchronicities.

In some chapters of this book I have prompted you to make notes and reflect. You might also find that you vehemently disagree with some of the comments I make—wonderful—I am pushing buttons for you, and it's a good idea to record your thoughts and feelings about the emotions that come up for you as you're reading. The point is, take the time to reflect. You might be amazed at what happens inside of you.

Ultimately, I aim to provoke thought and awareness, to create opportunities for discussion and reflection. It's up to you how far you choose to pursue these ideas personally.

This book also provides scripts for meditations which I hope you will find useful. You may photocopy or scan the pages with the meditation scripts as this makes using them more practical. You could record yourself or someone else reading the script with relaxing music playing in the background and then you can use them whenever you need to. You could use these meditations in small groups or simply read them through a few times yourself to familiarise the processes and then take yourself on the journey without the script. When you have completed the meditation, note how you are feeling. If something significant occurred, make a note in your journal.

*   *   *

CHAPTER ONE

Why do pagans need to know this stuff?

It's not only pagans, it's anyone interested in the healing arts, but for purpose of this book, I have focussed my attention on those who have chosen a 'pagan path' or indeed just a 'pagan' label in their life.

Why do pagans need to develop in the healing arts, why should they be aware of energy? In order to answer this question I need to first ask another . . . what is Paganism?

For me, being pagan is a lifestyle, it's about honouring Mother Earth, living in the cycle of the seasons, co-creating with nature, experiencing the essence of nature in all its forms, trees, animals, herbs, flowers, plants, but people are also part of nature. Paganism to me is also about daily spiritual practice. I believe that part of my role as a pagan is to help to heal the planet and those who live on her, to use the gifts nature has given us, e.g. herbs and flowers, plants and food to feed and heal our bodies and that of the earth herself. Therefore developing in the healing arts, in whatever tradition may best suit the individual, is one of the essential ingredients to what being pagan is all about, for me at least. And yet so many pagans are unaware of energy, how to manifest, how to protect and how to heal themselves and others.

I have used the word 'Pagan' here as an umbrella term to cover all traditions, labels and paths, from the Celtic to the Wiccan and back again. Essentially the techniques in this book can support anyone wishing to develop as a healer or to pursue their personal spiritual practice. So when I refer to 'pagans' I mean anyone reading this book, regardless of your faith, religion, background or culture. It's just that my motivating reason for writing this book was seeing the huge gaps in awareness, especially in some of the pagan community. More recently however, I have noticed things have started to change, as more people are opening up spiritually in their personal growth and development.

I have been to many pagan events and conferences and seen people who 'dress up' as pagan. What do I mean? I mean they have 'the pagan uniform'. They might wear black velvet or clad themselves with a purple cloak they may sport an array of beautifully designed tattoos or various body piercings. They wear pentacles and plenty of gothic jewellery. Are they pagan because they look this way?

Maybe they are—maybe their lifestyle choices are 'pagan' as much as their outfits are, maybe they do meditate, understand energy work, eat an animal free diet and know the names of trees and what herbs are good for what ailments, but my experience has largely shown that this is not the case. Am I simply stereotyping, making judgements based on what people look like? Perhaps I am, but isn't that what the wearers of these outfits want me to do? I do not have a problem with people wearing whatever they choose to wear; in fact, I support a person's right to be whoever they choose to be. The point I am making is that being pagan is not about the outfits or indeed the type of music, books or art enjoyed by the person, but by their regular Spiritual Practice.

I personally struggle with all the paraphernalia that comes with paganism (usually Wicca—although not always) and there's plenty of it to explore. Wands and cauldrons, crystals and athames . . . but are they simply there to look good, on the shelf to look impressive, or to be used practically?

Do pagans have ritual knives so that they can lovingly harvest the lavender to make ointment, or use a cauldron to collect up the calendula petals to make a cream for nappy rash? Or do these objects gather dust on an unused altar somewhere in the house because they are cool, and because witches *need* them?

You may consider that I am being a bit harsh, but there is a point to my comments. So many pagans are unaware of energy. So many pagans are unfamiliar with the power of healing. And many more pagans are unaware of the benefits of knowing about nature's gifts to us. BUT worse than just being unaware of these things, some pagans are actually creating dangerous situations and inviting entities and unhelpful energy into their bodies and auras, through unprotected and foolish rituals.

In the early days of my learning about healing and being a 'new' pagan, I read many books on rituals and one such ritual, "drawing down the moon", which I understand to be a common ceremony to undertake, was suggested, and so without any real understanding of energy, what I was doing, or the consequences of my ritual, I used the book I had read to do this ritual (I'm not going to tell you what I did as I do not want to encourage anyone else to do such a foolish thing.) I had an experience that was for sure, I felt things entering my body and had chest pains for an hour or so, then, I spent the next week being unable to sleep at night, I was exhausted and starting to get really ill! I visited my healer friend for help. She knew straight away what I had done, before I had even had the chance to tell her. I had unknowingly (although I did know because I'd invited them) 'drawn down' entities from somewhere, either the moon, night or sky energy, but low level entities (beings) for certain, which had come into my energy field and were playing havoc with my system. I had a healing session and was able to clear off the unhelpful energy I had invited in. That night I slept like a log.

Many pagans and people generally are unaware of the energy that is out there in the universe and yet proceed without caution to 'invite' these energies into their lives, homes and bodies. My experience was by no means serious, but over the years and since that time, I have worked with people who have opened up to unhelpful and low level entities and as a result their lives had been devastated. It's not appropriate to give specific case studies here, but suffice to say that I have spent more time doing healing sessions with damaged pagans than any other group of people I know. A pentacle will not protect you from energies that you invite in!

I know a lot of pagans who do *not* know how to ground their energy, who have no idea how to centre themselves (or even what that means) or how to balance their energy and who definitely have no idea about chakras, auras and how to channel safely, or attune. So instead of ranting, I'm going to explain it all—here, in this book. If you're pagan (and even if you're not) please read on. If I'm "teaching granny to suck eggs" then great—you're obviously a

THE HEALING POWER OF THE GODDESS; A PRACTICAL APPROACH FOR PAGANS
DEVELOPING IN THEIR SPIRITUAL PRACTICE AND THE HEALING ARTS

17

well-rounded, peaceful, secure, happy and healed individual who's equipped to offer healing to others . . . brilliant, this planet needs as many people like that as she can get!

So where do we begin?

I suggest we explore what healing actually is and how it works.

*   *   *

CHAPTER TWO

What's all this healing lark then?

What is healing?

What comes into your mind when you read the word "*healing*"?

Just take a moment to reflect on that word 'healing'.

What do you see in your mind's eye?

What impression do you get?

How do you feel?

The word 'healing' conjures up different images for different people and can even bring up specific emotions. I am often amazed at the variety of impressions that people get when I say that word and ask them for feedback. Of course, this largely depends upon their experiences and beliefs. Before I launch into sharing some of these impressions with you, I want you to take a moment to reflect on the impression that you get. So here it is again, what comes into your mind when you read the word "healing"?

Some people think of doctors as healers, or nurses and a very physical approach to healing e.g. wounds getting healed or broken bones healing up and knitting back together. Some people think of alternative healing and might see in their mind's eye a healing couch with a person laid on it receiving healing. There are many ideas about what healing is and how it works.

So, for the purpose of this book, I am going to explore several healing traditions, some of which are very energetic and more to do with internal and emotional healing, others are practical and can cover more physical ailments and the use of nature to help heal.

Reiki:

Often when people think of healing arts, they think of Reiki and I can see why this is the case, however, it is only one of the many traditions and approaches which can be adopted. I will start by considering the role of Reiki and move onto other approaches that can be safely adopted to facilitate healing.

According to William Rand's (1991) definition; "Reiki (pronounced 'ray-key') is a Japanese technique for stress reduction and relaxation that also promotes healing. It was rediscovered by Dr. Mikao Usui in the early 1900's. Reiki is administered by 'lying on of hands' and techniques such as this have been practiced for thousands of years." p.1

According to Bronwen and Frans Stiene (2005); The system of Reiki is a method of working with energy that allows the body to clear itself leaving you feeling lighter, healthier and happier" p.3

There is only one point to the latter definition that I actually agree with and that is that Reiki is 'a method of working', that is all—a method and not the only one. In this book I present other healing techniques which I consider to be more powerful, safer, effective and beneficial than the system of Reiki. I will explain why now.

An Apprenticeship Approach to Reiki:

Despite being a Reiki practitioner (and I have studied and experienced Reiki for more than 10 years), I do have some concerns about the Reiki system and how it is 'taught' in the west. For instance, a person may receive a Reiki attunement during a weekend course and so consider they are a healer. I can see the potential dangers with this concept and believe that development in healing and energy work is the responsibility of the practitioner, pagan or not.

I like to use the analogy of fire. Reiki, like fire, is a neutral energy that can be tapped into (when attuned) to heal. Reiki can also be used to cleanse and energise. In much the same way that fire can be used to purify, give energy for cooking, heating and light, so Reiki can be used for good. On the flip side, in the same way that fire can damage, destroy and burn, so too can the power of Reiki energy if used ignorantly. I have seen many situations where people have been 'burned' as they are working with energies they do not have enough experience with.

In this book there are several examples suggested for how to protect yourself and your client from these potential dangers. The key to success is the channel, the facilitator, the healer. Are they familiar with the energy and do they have the knowledge to facilitate the power of Reiki safely? Would you hand over a box of matches or a lighter to a small child with little experience of fire?

I have been to festivals and events and seen people attuned in a weekend, to "master level". Can a person be a developed healer after a weekend or even two weekends? I think not and I know not.

Personally I feel that Reiki development and training should be an apprenticeship approach. How can a person be competent in a healing art in a weekend? A healing art that has taken years to learn, develop and master? They simple can't be.

Real development requires practice, experience, wider reading and understanding of energy and people, attending groups for spiritual development and meditation and being open to learning and growing personally while also self-healing. A practitioner must surely be doing their own healing work and developing their spiritual practice. As far as I am concerned, having an attunement does not make anyone a master at anything—how can it?

I am not suggesting that pagans should all become Reiki Masters; in fact the opposite is true. But, whenever I try to discuss healing and energy work with fellow pagans I often hear the same response "Oh I have done Reiki" or "I am a Reiki Master." That type of comment. My desire to encourage pagans in general to be more aware of the energy they are working with has nothing to do with Reiki.

There are other traditions that people can opt to develop in, including; Angelic Reiki, Spiritual Healing, Theta Healing, Therapeutic Massage, Emotional Freedom Technique and the list goes on.

I am not even suggesting that pagans need or ought to develop in all these healing crafts, but I will say this;

Do you know what energy you are dealing with in your rituals?

Do you know what entities you are calling upon when you practice in magic?

Do you know how your body is doing, physically, spiritually, emotionally?

Do you have a sense of your own personal energy field and wellbeing?

How can you develop this? Simple, read on!

<u>Spiritual Healing:</u>

My preferred 'hands on healing' tradition is Spiritual Healing. This approach requires the healer to attune (plug into source energy) each time they work on a client; unlike Reiki where one attunement allows the healer to tap into energy whenever they like.

Spiritual Healing requires the healer to attune to the client each time they are working with them, opening themselves as a channel to 'source', 'divine light', 'God' or whatever label is preferred by the healer/client each time they give a treatment. I visualise this process in my mind's eye as a triangle. I attune to the client and their energy field while at the same time, I connect with Source, Divine Spirit Energy (I will explain how shortly) and I also open my client directly to Source Energy. This method insures that I am not using my own energy to heal.

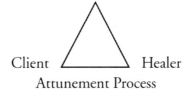

Source Energy
(Divine Spirit)

Client   Healer
Attunement Process

I have seen this happening with Reiki practitioners, who use their own energy as they are simply not attuning to the client each time. For whatever reason; the practitioner has not got clear channels, meridians and chakras themselves, and so the flow of Reiki energy is hindered and so they use their own energy, then they wonder why they feel so depleted and sick. How often does the Reiki master who is attuning the new practitioner actually check that the Reiki energy is flowing properly in them? Using Reiki energy requires regular practice and self-healing too!

Often Reiki practitioners do not protect themselves. This is because they believe that Reiki is safe, and that is their security. But what about the client's energy, is that safe? Has the client got entities or unwanted energy that could transfer? Do you know that for sure? As far as I am concerned protection is always needed. I will explain why and how.

<u>Why should I 'plug in' each time?</u>

Everyone is different and we all have different energy—in fact our energy levels change throughout the day. This can depend on the emotions we experience, the food we eat and who we are with. By taking the time to attune to your client, you are sensing their energy. You are taking the time to ensure that you are channelling effectively and not using your own energy—which can become depleted, and to ensure that you and the client are protected.

With practice, this attunement process only takes a few seconds. In this chapter, I set out how to attune and ensure that you are channelling source energy and not your own. When you read this initially, you may feel as though it's a long, complex and drawn out approach, however, over time and with practice, it becomes easier and more natural, until suddenly you are grounding, centering, protecting without too much effort.

My analogy is driving a car. When a person first learns to drive they have so many things to think about; mirror signal, manoeuvre as well as the other road users and not to mention having an awareness of where they are going. After some experience of driving, it is easier to get in to the car and only think consciously about where to go. The driving techniques themselves become automatic. This is the same with Spiritual Healing. Initially, a healer will be visualising their connection to 'source', attuning with the client, placing protection around themselves and their client and grounding and centering as well. Before long, this will become a natural procedure and the healing energy will flow without difficulty. The process of attunement is still taking place but the healer can go through these processes without thinking too much about them consciously. Just as with driving, we soon arrive at our destination and we can often have very little recollection about the process we took, having got there. The attunement and healing process becomes much like this over time.

Grounding:

This word is bounded about so frequently to mean a variety of things. For the purpose of this book I define 'being grounded' to mean "being connected solidly with mother earth by ensuring a connection of our physical body to the ground."

After meditation or healing or any form of spiritual practice that takes us into an alpha state* we can sometimes feel floaty or heady. To prevent this from happening we can ensure that we are well

---

*   alpha state - the state of relaxation and peaceful awakefulness, associated with prominent brain wave activity.

grounded before we start. I will explain a simple visualisation to demonstrate this.

Grounding is a way of securing our physical bodies to the earth and plugging into earth energy. We can use visualisation techniques to do this: e.g. imagining roots coming out of our feet and growing down into the ground. The energy from the earth can be drawn up through the roots and into our physical bodies—just like trees do with the nutrients of the soil.

Why is it important that we ground ourselves?

- brings 'life' in matter and to enable us to bring our healing abilities into the physical body

- increases balance and stability in our physical and our emotional state

- brings strength and protection

- helps in creating a bridge between spirit and matter

- provides an outlet making the release (of energy) easier

- allows the attainment of higher spiritual levels

If you find that after spiritual work you do feel light headed or dizzy, then there are many ways to ensure that you become grounded again. Here are few suggestions to get you started:

- stamp your feet

- eat and drink something

- put your roots back in the earth

- lay on the floor and connect your entire body to earth

- breath slowly and deeply while focusing on your feet

Grounding Visualisation:

Before starting any healing and energy work or meditation, try this visualisation.

Take a few deep breaths.

In your mind's eye, see roots growing out of your feet and burrowing deep, moving down into the ground, spreading far and wide into the centre of mother earth herself.

Notice how firmly connected you are to the earth and how solid it makes you feel.

Breathe in and out again with steady and slow breaths.

You are now grounded.

The more you practice this technique the easier it will become.

Healing Energy from Mother Earth:

Once your roots are well established in the earth, then you can visualise the red healing earth energy drawing up through your roots and into your body. As you breathe in, see this red healing light enter your body, coming up your legs and cleansing all your energy centres, while also refreshing your physical body. See your entire body filled with the powerful, energising, cleansing energy given freely from Mother Earth. How does this makes you feel? Notice any sensations in your body. You can tap into this healing earth energy whenever you need a boost.

Centering:

The term 'being centred' is also banded about and used to describe a variety of ideas. For the purpose of this book, I am using the term to mean "aligning all chakras (also called energy centres) bringing the appropriate balance for the body right now".

Centering yourself is an important process because it ensures that your energy centres are balanced and aligned, which is essential if you want your rituals, magic and energy work to be effective. This centering process can also be done using visualisation techniques. Centering is also about being focused and being present. Right Now!

Centering Technique:

Once your roots are securely established in mother earth then as you breathe in, draw up the earth energy through your roots, into your legs and into your first chakra, the root chakra.

You may see this as a red centre or flower. Allow the energy to cleanse and balance this chakra. Then draw the energy up through to the sacral chakra, you may see this as an orange centre or flower, once this chakra has been aligned then move your attention to the solar plexus, which you may see as a yellow centre of flower, allow this centre to be cleansed by the healing light from the earth before moving onto the heart centre, which you may see as a green, or in some cases, pink flower. Once this centre has been balanced and aligned with the healing energy from Mother Earth, move your attention to the throat chakra, which you may see as a blue centre or flower and then to the third eye in the middle of your brow, you may see this centre as a purple, violet or indigo colour and finally draw the energy all the way from your roots, through all your chakras, to the crown centre, situated at the top of your head. You may see this as a white, silver or gold flower.

Once the earth energy has cleansed all of your chakras they are aligned and balanced, you are now what I call 'centred'.

This may seem like a long-winded process and time consuming and the first few times that you do it, it may feel like being a learner driver as I said previously, but with practice you will be able to ground and centre yourself in a matter of seconds, literally, as you think it—it's done.

Protection:

This is the most critical part of the process and often the part that people tend to forget, or worse still, don't realise they should include, when they are channelling energy. You can choose to visualise protection anyway you like. I tend to feel that there are different types of protection for different occasions, much like in life.

At one time we may only need an apron to stop getting flour on our clothes, another time we need a hard hat to protect our skull from falling debris. The same principle applies to healing and energy work. This includes times when you are doing rituals and magic. The type of protection you choose to adopt will be determined by the type of work you are doing. Here are some suggestions;

1.) When channelling healing, I like to visualise a bubble of white light around myself like a force field, only love and healing can get through the filter. I also visualise a bubble of light around the client I am giving healing to. Some people like to use an egg as their protection. Others see a spinning disc moving all around their energy field, with negativity bouncing off the discs and still the healing can filter through. Whatever visualisation technique you like can be effective here, as long as you have the intention for protection.

2.) Sometimes there are occasions when stronger protection is required. If I am in a situation where I am in close proximity to lots of people, where their energy can affect me, then I may visualise armour. For example, on the tube train in London I tend to see the steel of the armour all the way around me, close to my skin and covering my head and body, protecting me from unwanted energy. Once I am out of that situation then I resort back to a bubble of light or an egg. I wouldn't choose to have armour on for long periods of time, but a stronger protection can prove useful in certain circumstances.

3.) Sometimes only a part of your body will need protection. For example, you could visualise having a shield in front of your heart centre or solar plexus in emotional situations.

4.) Other traditions call on angels, archangels and ascended masters for protection.

5.) Some people like to use objects for protection, herbs, crystals, symbols, stones, runes and so on.

Although I can appreciate that these objects may be beneficial for some people, I prefer to use visualisation techniques as I always have my mind with me and I can tap into this power whenever I need it. "Energy follows thought." What I think about, I create. If my intention is for protection and I see a white ball of light surrounding and protecting me, then I have created that level of protection for my energy system, without the need for objects.

I can recall a situation recently when I was asked for advice about a stall at a pagan event. The lady was worried that something might be stolen while she wasn't there. I was surprised by her concern generally, but simply said, put protection on it. Her answer was, "I haven't got any of my stuff with me". Stuff, what stuff? We don't need 'stuff' to create protection. I simply said "intention is everything, visualise your protection, 'Energy follows thought'." It amazes me that so many pagans are unaware in their own spiritual practice how to actually protect themselves and their homes.

Find the protection that suits the situation, but know that whenever you are involved with ritual, energy work or any of the healing arts, protection is essential.

I consider protection in greater detail in the next chapter.

Channelling Source Energy:

Once you are grounded, centred and protected (mirror, signal, manoeuvre) you are ready to drive, by channelling healing energy for another person, for yourself, for animals, for nature, for Mother Earth, whoever and whatever needs it!

Now you have put your roots in the ground (you are grounded) you have drawn up earth energy and aligned your chakras (you are centred) and you have visualised protection around yourself, in whatever form is appropriate for you at this time. Now you are ready to channel in the light.

Channelling Light:

In your mind's eye, see your crown chakra (centre at the top of your head) opening up, like a flower, or a trap door, or a funnel, whatever works best for you.

As you breathe in, allow the bright healing light energy from source to pour down into your crown, visualise it filling your body with light.

The light can fill all your energy centres and cleanse each chakra bringing healing and balance to your own body. The light runs through your limbs and out of your palm chakras. It can help if you rub your hands together to stimulate your palm chakras.

(Notice how intuitively, if a child hurts themselves, we suggest rubbing the injured part. Perhaps the rubbing is to stimulate the palms and get the healing energy flowing? I would urge you to stay with it and not rush to move away from the injury but to allow the healing to have time, especially with children.)

This healing light energy is then flowing through you and out of your hands, so whoever you place your hands onto, can also benefit from the power and healing of this source energy you have tapped into. This is Spiritual Healing.

Plugging into source energy and channelling that light through your body and to others. Anyone can do this. Once you have attuned to your client and followed the basic procedure, ground, centre, protect, channel—you are healing! You do not have to be attuned to Reiki in order to be able to channel healing light energy in this way.

Following, is a script for a meditation to enable you to ground, centre and protect. This can be done in preparing for healing, ritual magic or self-healing as a way to cleanse and prepare the body as well as close it down safely afterwards. The following script could be used in a group setting or you could record yourself reading it with appropriate music in the background for your own personal meditations. Alternatively, you could read it through a few times until you are comfortable with the approach and then do the visualisation in your mind's eye from memory to get the gist of the process.

The guided medications and visualisations in this book may be photocopied or scanned to make using them more practical.

*   *   *

Guided Meditation for Grounding, Centering and Protection

Find a comfortable position, either lying down or sitting in a straight
back chair, whichever feels best to you today. Take a few nice deep
breaths, bringing your awareness fully to the present moment. Let go
of any busy thoughts preventing you from tapping into your inner
essence. See a bubble of white light surrounding you completely.
Know that when you are surrounded by this beautiful bubble of
white, light you are protected.

Bring your attention to the soles of your feet and in your mind's
eye, see roots growing out of our body and connecting with mother
earth, growing deep down into the earth as far and wide and deep as
you see them grow. As you breathe in, the red healing earth energy
is drawn up through your roots, like a nourishing nutrient for your
soul and physical body. Begin to focus on your root chakra at the
base of your spine, see it as a beautiful flower opening. As you breathe
in the red healing earth energy, it is drawn up into your base chakra
and the flower opens and is clear and bright.

Now focus your attention on your sacral chakra, located between
your root chakra and your navel, see this as a beautiful orange flower.
As you breathe in the red healing earth energy, it is drawn up into
your sacral chakra and the flower opens and is clear and bright.

Now focus your attention on your solar plexus, see this as a beautiful yellow flower. As you breathe in the red healing earth energy, it is drawn up into your solar chakra and the flower opens and is clear and bright.

Now focus your attention on your heart centre, see this as a beautiful green flower. As you breathe in the red healing earth energy, it is drawn up into your heart chakra and the flower opens and is clear and bright.

Now focus your attention on your throat centre, see this as a beautiful blue flower. As you breathe in the red healing earth energy, it is drawn up into your throat chakra and the flower opens and is clear and bright.

Now focus your attention on your third eye, see this as a beautiful purple flower. As you breathe in the red healing earth energy, it is drawn up into your third eye chakra and the flower opens and is clear and bright.

Finally, focus your attention on your crown chakra; see this as a beautiful white flower. As you breathe in the red healing earth energy, it is drawn up into your crown chakra and the flower opens and is clear and bright. Now you are ready to open your crown and receive the healing light from Divine Spirit.

As you breathe in, allow the golden light from the highest and brightest beings of love, light and healing, to pour down through your crown centre filling your entire body. This light permeates all the cells of your body bringing you healing and peace on all levels. Take a moment to sit in this energy.

Know that your chakras are balanced and you are centered and protected.

When you are ready, bring your awareness back to your crown chakra and close it tightly shut. You may choose to see this as a trap door or a tap you can turn off. Now allow your chakras to close to a safe and appropriate level for you at this time. Bring your awareness back to the room, open your eyes, stretch, yawn and smile, feeling refreshed and renewed.

*   *   *

Guided meditation for self-healing

Find a comfortable position, either lying down or sitting in a straight back chair, whichever feels best to you today. Take a few nice deep breaths, bringing your awareness fully to the present moment. Let go of any busy thoughts preventing you from tapping into your inner essence.

Now I'll begin the guided meditation, and as I mention each body part I invite you to bring your awareness to it and relax it as deeply as you can. As you scan your body, if you encounter tension anywhere simply use the power of your mind to melt it away, as easily as warm water melts ice.

Starting at the top of your head, relax your scalp completely. Feel the skin of your forehead and temples relax. Allow your eye muscles to release, your jaw to soften, and let your ears, nose and chin, teeth tongue and gums relax. Now, just let this peaceful feeling flow down your neck. Feel it sooth your throat and dissolve any tension on contact as it glides down to your shoulders, upper arms, forearms, wrists and hands.

Let this peaceful sensation of relaxation begin to fill your torso. Feel it relax your chest, giving your heart more room to grow more expansive; more loving, giving and forgiving. Soften your tummy muscles and let this relaxation penetrate even deeper, releasing any tension from your internal organs.

Now let it wrap around you, enveloping you in love and peace as it softens all the back muscles all the way down to the base of the your spine. Continue to breathe in deep, fluid breaths. Breathe in health, happiness and harmony; breathe out any tension, toxins, worries or disease, allowing anything that does not serve you to leave your body.

Send this peaceful feeling into your hips and buttocks. Let it glide down your thighs, relaxing your legs completely as it flows down to your knees, calves, ankles and feet. Allow any remaining tension from anywhere in your body to flow out your toes, leaving your whole body feeling very comfortable, peaceful and relaxed.

Continue to breathe deep relaxing breaths, feeling your stomach rise on the inhale and fall on the exhale. Notice how the air feels cooler as you breathe in, and warmer as you breathe out. Now, imagine a golden glowing ball of light about a foot above the crown of your head. On an inhalation, breathe that light in through the top of your head through the centre line of your body, right down to the tailbone. On the exhalation, breathe that light back up the way it came and out the top of your head. We'll do this three times, to begin to balance and align your chakras.

Begin to focus on your root chakra at the base of your spine and visualise a vibrant red glowing ball of light, or if you prefer, imagine a red crystal, flower or fruit. This chakra brings health, security and dynamic presence. Notice the petals, are they clear and bright? If they need more light, breathe in the golden light allowing it to your chakras and cleanse your red flower making it clear and bright. Feel it empower you as it connects you to earth energies. You're radiating power and vitality. Breathe the colour red in and out and see yourself living your healthy ideal, feeling happy and grateful for radiant health and boundless energy, weighing your perfect weight with a strong, balanced immune system. Feel how good it feels to have all the energy you need to do all the things you love to do. You feel so grateful for this magnificent body that moves so freely and well and looks so good. Feel yourself healthier than you've ever felt before. Now let this vibrant red chakra continue to glow and spin as you move up to your sacral chakra, located between your root chakra and your navel.

Here, see a radiant glowing orange ball of light. This chakra holds the energy of money, power, sexuality and creativity. Breathe in a rich beautiful orange color and feel it bring the gifts of being happy, enthusiastic, sexually fulfilled, prosperous and abundant. See yourself experiencing true wealth on every level, being grateful for the abundance in your life now, and imagine riches flowing to you in expected and unexpected ways. Let this chakra continue to glow and spin as you move up to your solar chakra located a few inches above your navel.

Here, see a beautiful sunny yellow glowing ball of light, or visualise a lemon or a sunflower. As you breathe in a vibrant yellow colour, feel it expand your joy, self-worth and personal power. See yourself successful and deeply fulfilled in your dream job. Feel the glowing yellow chakra empower you as you move up to your heart chakra at the centre of your chest, and visualise a beautiful emerald green or a soft pink glowing ball of light.

This is the chakra of love for yourself and others. Let it glow, bringing gifts of compassion, self-acceptance, and the ability to love deeply. Breathe in pink or green and let these feelings expand, seeing yourself living in perfect harmony with everyone in your life. Let it fill you with gratitude for this opportunity to live in this wonderful world. Feel your heart swell with compassion and forgiveness for yourself and others. Now allow this chakra to continue to glow and spin and gently move up to your throat chakra located at your neck, visualising a beautiful blue colour. This chakra enables you to communicate with truth and wisdom and express yourself with confidence. Breathing blue in and out, see yourself happily expressing your uniqueness through a creative outlet you enjoy such as singing, dancing, playing a sport, anything you do for fun. Let this chakra continue to glow and spin and gently move up to your third eye chakra located at the centre of your forehead.

See a beautiful deep purpley blue indigo coloured glowing ball of light. As it glows it expands your imagination, psychic abilities, inner knowing and wisdom. Feel fully supported by the Universe as you pursue your personal growth goals, happily following your highest path. See yourself living your ideal in the personal growth area of your life, whatever that means to you.

Now allow this indigo light to continue to glow and spin as you gently move up to your crown chakra at the top of your head. This is the chakra of spirituality, thought, and service to others. Breathe in violet or white, gold or silver and let this chakra glow as it brings gifts of self-knowledge, spiritual connection and bliss. See yourself living in wisdom and awareness, surrendering into divine love, joyfully contributing to the world in the way most meaningful for you. Let this chakra glow and spin as you bring your awareness back to the golden glowing light above your head. As you breathe in, allow this golden light from the highest and brightest beings of love, light and healing to pour down through your crown centre filling your entire body. This light permeates all the cells of your body bringing you healing and peace on all levels.

Take a moment to sit in this energy. Know that your chakras are balanced and you are centered and protected. As this Divine Light floods your entire body, you can receive healing for all aspects and on all levels, whatever you need at this time.

When you are ready, bring your awareness back to your crown chakra and close it tight shut, you may choose to see this as a trap door or a tap you can turn off. Now allow your chakras to close to a safe and appropriate level for you at this time. Bring your awareness back to the room, open your eyes, stretch, yawn and smile, feeling refreshed and renewed.

*   *   *

Distance Healing:

If we are unable to physically get our hands on someone to give them healing, then we can send the energy out to them distantly. There may be occasions when it's not possible to work directly with a person. Perhaps they are far away, or they are in hospital for example. We can still be active in sending healing energy and loving thoughts to them. Healing can also be sent to situations and events, to the past and the future, I will cover this in more detail shortly.

In pagan circles, I have read and seen so called healing rituals that are either useless or dangerous; from one extreme to another. The pointless ones I can cope with, although it is a shame because if a person is prepared to make the effort to ask for healing for a loved one, then it makes sense to be effective in that process. Alternatively, I have witnessed outrageously dangerous rituals that have the potential to cause more damage to a person who is already sick. It is this type of affair that I hope to see a reduction in.

Sending healing energy to others is a fairly easy and safe process and it certainly does not require any extra tools, equipment, crystals, proxy dolls or any other such gumph.

Distance Healing:

How can we send healing to people?

There are several ways to do this but the following list contains the most effective, quickest and easiest ways to send out healing.

- Visualise the life-sized person seated in front you and complete a healing treatment

- Visualise a group of people or places in miniature and put them in a protective circle of light in front of you and see healing light energy beaming down on the circle

- Write names down with the INTENTION of sending healing to those people—this is how the healing book works

- Use an affirmation/statement e.g. I am sending healing to . . . right now, may they receive the energy of this beautiful healing light.

Earth Healing:

Also send healing to the earth and all her creatures—visualise the earth as a miniature planet spinning on her axis and regenerating her energies, with the healing light beaming down on the planet.

Guided meditation for distant and earth healing

Find a comfortable position, either lying down or sitting in a straight back chair, whichever feels best to you today. Take a few nice deep breaths, bringing your awareness fully to the present moment. Let go of any busy thoughts preventing you from tapping into your inner essence.

Now, bring your attention to your feet and see the roots growing deep, deep down into Mother Earth. Open each chakra one by one cleansing each one with earth energy. As you breathe in the healing red light from the earth is drawn up your roots and into each chakra bringing a sense of balance and wholeness. When you reach your crown chakra allow this to open and white healing light flood your entire body. Now you are receiving healing you may also give this out to others. Think of people you know who need this energy right now and those on your healing list, and ask that they might also receive this beautiful energy right now.

In your mind's eye see the planet as a miniature version in front of you, spinning on her axis and see the bright white light shining down on the planet so that Mother Earth can be restored and replenished to her former glory. You may also choose to 'beam' the energy from your palms to the planet at the same time.

When you are ready, bring your awareness back to your crown chakra and close it tightly shut. You may choose to see this as a trap door or a tap you can turn off. Now allow your chakras to close to a safe and appropriate level for you at this time. Bring your awareness back to the room, open your eyes, stretch, yawn and smile, feeling refreshed and renewed.

*   *   *

Healing for situations and events past and future

There may be circumstances we have experienced which continue to haunt us. Having healing in the present is one way to help move on. However, I have also worked with people to heal a past event by "going back" in the mind's eye to that time, seeing it, feeling it, noticing the emotions and then sending healing to that time, situation, person or child. This can also work for future scenarios. If for example you know that you have a dentist appointment a week on Tuesday, you can send energy out to that time. Maybe seeing yourself sat in the dentist's chair and then visualise; sending healing energy to you as you sit in that chair. See yourself feeling relaxed and at ease, clam and peaceful. Focus only on the emotions you wish to experience. When the time comes for you to be there—you can relax back knowing the energy is already there for you. Breathe in the healing and feel it flow throughout your appointment.

*   *   *

CHAPTER THREE

Keeping the monsters at bay

This chapter will focus upon the need for protection and suggest several techniques in greater detail. This is the main area that I feel pagans need to become more aware. Having said that, just being aware is not enough, action needs to be taken to ensure the safety of your personal energy field, your physical body and your home. An excellent resource on the topic of psychic protection and given in much more detail, is a book entitled "The Witch's Shield" (see bibliography for details) I am also keen on healers having a book called "Dancing with the Devil and you Channel in the Light" which I feel should be in every healer or alternative therapist's toolkit of resources. This book discusses entities, how they can affect us as how to clear them from the body and from homes and buildings. For the purpose of this chapter I am focussing purely on protection from the point of view of developing in the healing arts and protection when participating in or indeed watching, magical rituals.

Mind Matters:

The true key to protection is our thoughts. If we give a situation, issue or problem lots of energy by talking about it or thinking about it negatively, then we are also giving that situation, issue or problem its power. Remember 'energy follows thought'. What we think about, we create. We are creating our experience, that's how magic works. Our thoughts and actions are the power for manifesting our reality. When it comes to protection, often we are making matters worse with our thinking and we forget the magical power of words too.

The Power of Words:

We may think that our words are simply 'figures of speech'; however, words carry vibrational energy, which is why we use words in rituals and in spells. Think about prayer for a moment. What is prayer? It's our thoughts made into words. And yet, so often I hear people saying things that are detrimental to their health and wellbeing. For example: "I'm sick and tired of . . .", "She'll be the death of me . . .", "I can't afford it . . ." and so on. This type of negative speaking and thinking easily diminishes our personal power and affects our energy levels. We will be ineffective in our protection, energy work, and spiritual practice if we remain unaware of our thoughts and the power of our words. Later on I discuss *manifestation* in more detail and suggest ways in which we can create the life we want for ourselves.

Send Love:

If you are in a challenging situation, or a specific person is causing a problem and you need protection, then send them love. Maybe send out healing to them distantly, and bless them. This is not always an easy process but the benefits can be noticed immediately. When we send out positive energy to others, this also has an immediate effect on our state of mind and energy system. We remain protected from harm, physically and emotionally as well as energetically and spiritually.

Call in the Angels:

The Queen of everything Angelic is Doreen Virtue and if you have not had the pleasure of reading any of her books that I highly recommend that you source her material.

I am a believer in the power of angelic beings and the traditional healing method that I practice requires me to call upon the angels and archangels for assistance when protection or clearing is needed.

I have noticed that pagans (generally speaking) don't like to refer to angelic beings and consider angels a 'fluffy bunny' approach to pagan spirituality. I have heard wiccans say that Angels are 'airy fairy' and 'wishy washy' and of no use in their ritual spaces. I of course, disagree. Regardless of tradition, spiritual path, belief system or label, angelic energy is far from 'wet' or 'fluffy bunny'. Some of the most powerful healing experiences of my life have involved the energy, power and magic of the Angelic Realms and there is nothing 'wishy washy' about the sword that Archangel Michael cuts psychic cords with!

Whenever you need protection in a hurry, call in the Angels. Knowing the energies of the Angelic Realms by name can useful, but it's not essential, just have the intention and invite them, they will be there. For further reading, have a look at a book entitled, "The Lightworker's Way" by Doreen Virtue.

Chimney of Light:

We all have the opportunity to be plugged into spiritual energy should we wish to. One suggestion is to create a 'Chimney of Light'. This process gives us the opportunity to be connected with Mother Earth and Source Energy at the same time and leave the connection open safely. I have also established a Chimney of Light in my home as well as for my body. The opportunity here is to be able to release unwanted energy which can return to the light for transmutation easily, as the chimney is already established. To create this Chimney of Light, I have visualised a column of white light reaching right up into the 'heavens' and right down deep into the earth. Any unhelpful energy is instantly transmuted. Anything that passes through this light is cleansed and purified.

Space clearing:

There are many ways to ensure that your home, place of work or ritual space is clear of unwanted energy. Visualisation techniques such as the Chimney of Light can be used, or seeing in your mind's eye the room being filled with bright, white, sparkling light. Alternatively, there are more practical ways to clear spaces physically.

1. Smudging
2. Sound Bathing
3. Sacred Space Sprays
4. Water Cleansing

Smudging:

Our Native elders have taught us that before a person can be healed or heal another, one must be cleansed of any bad feelings, negative thoughts, bad spirits or negative energy—cleansed both physically and spiritually. This helps the healing to come through in a clear way, without being distorted or sidetracked by negative "stuff" in either the healer or the client. The elders say that all ceremonies, tribal or private, must be entered into with a good heart so that we can pray, sing, and walk in a sacred manner, and be helped by the spirits to enter the sacred realm.

Native people throughout the world use herbs to accomplish this. One common ceremony is to burn certain herbs, take the smoke in one's hands and rub or brush it over the body. Today this is commonly called "smudging." In Western North America the plant most frequently used in smudging is sage.

Sage: There are many varieties of sage, and most have been used in smudging. The botanical name for "true" sage is Salvia (e.g. *Salvia officinalis*, Garden Sage, or Salvia apiana, White Sage). It is interesting to note that Salvia comes from the Latin root salvare, which means "to heal." Sage is burned in smudging ceremonies to drive out bad spirits, feelings, or influences, and also to keep bad spirits from entering the area where a ceremony takes place. In Plains nations, the floor of the sweat lodge is frequently covered with sage, and participants rub the leaves on their bodies while in the sweat. Sage is also commonly spread on the ground in a lodge or on an altar where the pipe touches the earth. Some nations wrap their pipes in sage when they are placed in pipe-bundles, as sage is believed to purify the objects it is wrapped in.

To do a smudging ceremony, light the bunched up dried sage herb stick allowing the dried leaves to burn giving off the cleansing smoke. Blow out the flame. Use the smoke to cleanse the etheric body. Starting with the top of the head and work down the front and back of the aura with the intention of cleansing unwanted energy and drawing it down into the earth for transmutation. Sometimes, one person will smudge another, or even a whole group of people, using the stick, their hands full of smoke or a feather to lightly brush the smoke over the other people. When the smudging is complete, extinguish the smudge stick in a pot of sand, soil, grit or small stones. If water is used it will be very tricky to relight the stick in the future.

Sound bathing:

Using a Tibetan singing bowl or tingsha move around the space or person allow the sound to vibrate the energy of the room/person. It's useful to open a window to allow any unwanted energy to escape or visualise it being transmuted by the light. Sitting in the energy of these sounds, or indeed crystal singing bowls is a good way to cleanse the energy body and bring healing.

Sacred Space Sprays:

Sacred Space Spray can be used when cleansing a room of negative energy. Energy in a room can become stagnant. It is also polluted by electrical equipment such as TVs, mobile phones and computers. Energy fragments left by people can also clutter the space. Sacred Space Sprays are designed to clear unwanted and stale energy, bringing a fresh and clean energy to the environment. These sprays are made from herbal and flower essences and water. Spray up into the air and especially into the corners or areas where energy flow can stop.

Water Cleansing:

Cleaning:

The obvious place to start is the physical act of cleaning a room. Use a bucket of warm water and a cloth to remove dust particles.

Avoid chemicals, sprays and dusters as these products tend to just move the dust around the room. If you are preparing a space for a ritual the first thing to do is clean the area. A physical cleanse is as important as an energetic clear out. I often add a squeeze of lemon juice to the bowl of water when cleaning. This keeps everything smelling fresh but not perfumed.

Water Bowl Cleansing:

This is a wonderful and very effective way to clear negative energy in a home or work place. Take a bowl of filtered and energised water and place it in the middle of the room. Make it your intention to visualise any negativity being drawn to this water. Leave it overnight. Don't let your pets drink it! The next day carefully empty the water into a drain outside. Do not be tempted to water plants with it as it will be saturated with energy. I have noticed that sometimes the water can smell stale after this process. Tip it away carefully.

Cleansing Crystals & Ritual Tools:

If you use crystals you will know the importance of cleaning them regularly. For ease we tend to use a running tap. I suggest that when possible you take your collection of crystals to a clean running stream and allow them to be cleansed by the waters, in a natural environment. You can do the same for any ritual tools you may use.

*   *   *

CHAPTER FOUR

Love Who I Am

Spiritual Practice:

Being pagan and being a healer is a lifestyle choice. Working on aspects of myself, is all part of that process. I am frequently amazed at how few people are doing their own personal healing work in their daily lives, as and when issues occur or emotions crop up. There are many ways to do this and I am not suggesting that healing is the only way to address personal challenges, although it is a good starting point.

A good way to check if we are engaging in regular, preferably daily spiritual practice is to actually take a look at ourselves. You could try using this acronym; LOVE WHO I AM as a way to reflect on your personal spiritual practice.

LOVE WHO I AM:

Love is a powerful word and it can be defined in many ways. For the purpose of this chapter I am using the word as an acronym to help me explain some important aspects of my spirituality and personal spiritual practice.

54

L—Listen
O—Observe
V—Visualise
E—Energy

The following pages encourage you to reflect on your own life and experiences as you read. To me, this is all part of your personal spiritual practice as you get to know yourself on all levels. Each section provides a challenge for you to consider. I suggest that you *create a personal journal* and make notes about your experiences, thoughts and feelings as you read. It is advisable to also write the date that you made the notes so that when you look back at your reflections, you can see how far you have come in your own personal and spiritual journey of growth and development.

Listen:

Listening to others:

It's easy to talk. Listening is more challenging. We have so much to say and so little time. When others are talking we are thinking about what we want to say next. We interrupt. We switch off. In the western world now, we pay people to listen to us. We employ counsellors and therapists to sit and listen to our 'stuff'. In the past, these discussions would have taken place within a family setting. Nowadays, do we really listen to our friends, family, spouses and children? In place of listening, do we prefer instead to give advice, suggest, compare and share our experiences? Sometimes we think we are listening when really we are trying to provide a solution. This is not listening. Sometimes we 'pretend' we are listening by making the right 'mmm' noises and nodding in appropriate places, but very often our minds are elsewhere.

Why do we need to listen to others anyway?

I feel that it is important for me to explain the benefits of listening. If you have not yet had the pleasure of reading "How to Win Friends and Influence People" written by Dale Carnegie, then I suggest that you do. This book explains how you will instantly be liked, appreciated, accepted and seen positively if you take the time to:

* become genuinely interested in other people

* become a good listener and encourage others to talk about themselves

* talk in terms of the *other* person's interests

* make the other person feel important

One way to ensure that the people who are close to you *feel* important is to make the time and have the willingness to listen to them. Hear *their* stuff. Avoid jumping in with things like; "that happened to me too when . . ." and launching into your own stories. It's easy to do but we need to stop.

Allow gaps, silence and space in conversations. It doesn't matter if no-body is talking. Gaps allow people the opportunity to say what it is they are thinking and feeling. It is tempting to fill the silences with pointless and meaningless chatter but it is not necessary.

Challenge:

Take time to listen to others. Don't talk about yourself at all today.
Be quiet. Listen to other people. Hear their stuff and see what you
notice. Then consider the following:

> How does it make you feel when listening to
> others?
> Is it difficult? Do you have to stop yourself
> interrupting?
> Were you tempted to bring the conversation round
> to you?

Consider:

> Who do you know who listens well?
> What makes them a good listener?
> Who do *you* go to if you need to talk?

Have you wanted to talk about an issue and approached a friend
or family member only to find that they are not really listening to
you? How did this make you feel?

Watch:

> Observe children with their parents.
> Try this when you're next in the supermarket.
> Are those parents really listening?
> How do you know? What did you notice?
> Was the child trying to communicate something?
> What was the response they got?

I suggest that you make some notes in your journal about your thoughts and experiences.

*   *   *

Listening to yourself:

Listening carefully to your inner voice is as important as listening to others. So often we get caught up in the 'rat race'. Our lives become a series of tasks; eat, work, sleep; and we forget to take the time to be still and listen. Knowing the difference between your mind's ongoing chatter and that inner voice of intuition is the crucial aspect.

My friend told me a recent story of her intuition giving her a prompt to "pick up a tissue". She failed to follow that inner voice and didn't put a tissue in her bag. Five minutes later while driving, she had a little nose bleed. Why didn't she listen to that inner voice? "I knew I was supposed to pick up a tissue, I nearly did, but then ignored it as I thought with my logical brain, 'I won't need that there are tissues at work'!" This example is not a life or death situation and my friend pulled into the petrol station to buy tissues.

What if we ignore these inner prompts in more serious situations? To start with the little things are important. We can become in tune with our bodies and our thoughts and in some cases save future pain and frustration. Stilling the chatter is the starting point for listening to your inner voice.

All the answers we could ever need are already within us. We just need to listen. Taking time out to be away from the TV, radio, mobile phones, computers or whatever the distraction is, and just being alone, in your own company.

This can initially be an uncomfortable place to be and you will notice the mind chatter hugely. Little conversations you have with yourself, scenarios you create, and worry you hold onto you. All that really exists in honesty, is the present; this moment, right now. There is no point in thinking about the past, it's been and gone. The future hasn't happened yet, so it's a waste of time worrying about that, so just be present and listen.

You can help to still the mind chatter by placing your tongue on the roof of your mouth. I find this really helps me to still the thoughts. If you find that thoughts are still coming, that's OK, just observe them and watch them go by. You can be detached from your thoughts. Your higher self is not the same as your brain, so it's possible to observe the crazy conversations, note them and let them go, like a passing breeze.

Some people like to use 'tools' to help them draw out their intuition, tarot or divination cards, dowsing rods and pendulums, all of which can be used, but I personally feel that they are not required, as nice as they can be.

For example; the concept of dowsing is that you already know the answer you are seeking and the muscles in your body can give you the response as you hold the pendulum, it gives you the answer because you already know it, deep inside you—the information you seek is already there. So I urge you to try to listen to yourself without the tools.

Challenge:

Take some time to sit still and reflect. Focus on your breathing.

Allow your thoughts to be still and quiet.

Observe your thoughts as they pass.

Can you hear that inner voice of intuition?

What is it saying to you?

Do you have a question to ask yourself?

Consider:

Do I listen to my intuition in my daily life?

Do I follow my intuition?

Watch:

Do you notice times when your inner voice is prompting you?

What do you do? Do you follow that instruction?

Does your logical mind 'kick in'?

I suggest that you make some notes in your journal

about your thoughts and experiences.

*   *   *

Listening to nature:

This statement is taken from a paper called; 'Sound—Medicine for the New Millennium'.

> "Human beings have been using sound to access deeper states of consciousness, expand awareness and heal the body for thousands of years. Chanting, toning, Tibetan singing bowls, Chinese meditation gongs, and mantras, are just a few examples of this use of sound. Today, with highly sophisticated technological equipment, we can not only observe the functioning of the body and the brain in unprecedented detail, but also measure the changes that take place in the mind and body in different states of consciousness and different states of health."
>
> Dr. Jeffrey D. Thompson, D.C., B.F.A.
> *http://www.neuroacoustic.com/newmil.html*

There are many sounds within nature that we can listen to in order to aid relaxation, and self healing. These include running water, dolphin and bird song or the wind in the trees. Although nowadays we can use CDs and sound tracks that have recorded nature, I'd like to suggest that you take some time to be with nature and listen to these sounds in the real environment. Research suggests that being in a relaxed state of consciousness, with the sounds of nature, can speed up the body's recovery process and aid healing.

Perhaps a visit to the woods, a stone circle, a beach or even a local park would provide the opportunity for you to listen to the healing sounds of nature. Personally I love water sounds and the crashing of ocean waves. I like to meditate with these sounds and visualise a cleansing process as I imagine that the stream, waterfall or lake is washing over me. I enjoy being at one with nature and feeling the rhythm of the earth. If you are unable to get outside easily then healing CDs with nature music may be an ideal starting point.

"Research projects in major universities across the country have explored the neurophysiology of meditation, deep relaxation states and mind/body interactions during healing. In one study a simple meditation technique used for 20 minutes a day caused profound changes in blood pressure, stress handling ability, immune response and feelings of well being—never mind using any kind of high-tech approach which could bring consciousness to very deep levels of relaxation. Using this technology as a daily tool for mind/body integration and stress reduction can have many positive benefits."

Dr. Jeffrey D. Thompson, D.C., B.F.A.
http://www.neuroacoustic.com/newmil.html

Listening to nature:

Challenge:

Visit somewhere beautiful where all you can hear is nature.

Sit on a blanket and relax in that environment.

Enjoy listening to the sound of nature. Try meditating in that environment.

Consider:

How do you feel? What did you hear? What did you notice?

Why did you choose that specific place? What was difficult?

Is there somewhere else you could visit where there are nature sounds?

Watch:

How does your body respond when sitting in nature?

Which sounds do you feel a real connection with?

Why do you think that is?

Which environment do you prefer? Beach? Woods? Park?

I suggest that you make some notes in your journal

about your thoughts and experiences.

*   *   *

Observe others:

As a child I was often told "don't worry about what others are doing, concentrate on your own endeavours". Now, as an adult and teacher I would urge the opposite to be the case. We can learn so much by watching people; observing behaviour, responses and actions. As an outsider looking in we are often able to see the 'bigger picture' and get an overall feel for a situation that we would otherwise not be aware of.

We have a lot to learn from children. Often we don't get (make) the time to observe them. I don't have children of my own but I have worked closely with them as an infant school teacher. In some ways, it's easier as an 'outsider' looking in, to see where children are coming from. Their 'imaginary' friends for example, so often dismissed, could they perhaps be angels, elementals or people who have passed over into spirit?

In my year 1 class, there was a little girl who was very intuitive. This child talked about being a (male) writer with long hair and using a quill to write with. She was able to describe people, places, smells and houses in great detail. Maybe she'd seen a programme on TV? Maybe she had a vivid imagination? Or maybe, she recalled a past life? At five she was herself a fantastically skilled writer.

Another child (also five years old) drew incredible pictures of people. He always used pencil crayons and he shaded over each person that he had drawn, with different colours. One particular day I heard another teacher telling this child to use colours 'properly' and to look carefully. She proceeded to say; "Jo isn't purple is he? He's got brown skin, now find a brown and colour him in properly. Look carefully at the colours and use the right ones." I wondered, as I watched this interaction, if this adult herself was "looking carefully".

Perhaps this child could see more than meets the eye? What was this child seeing at he looked at people?

This is just one example and I have experienced many throughout my teaching career. I learnt more from observing children than I think they ever learnt from me. I appreciate that in a fast pace world of busyness, routines and deadlines it is not always easy to stop and observe, but I urge you to take time to observe children. What is really happening may not be what you see at first glance.

Challenge:

When going about your daily business take some time to observe people and children.

Consider:

How do they behave? Are their actions what you would do? Why?

How do people communicate with each other?

How does this make you feel?

Watch:

Notice how the adults that you see locally interact with children.

Observe the tone of voice and body language used.

Notice how these same adults interact with each other.

Observe the tone of voice and body language used.

Do you think that there are varying degrees of respect in each situation?

I suggest that you make some notes in your journal

about your thoughts and experiences.

*   *   *

Observe yourself:

How often do you take notice of your own actions, feelings and behaviours? How frequently do you take the time to observe what you are doing in your life? Largely we are so engrossed in the things that we are doing that we fail to observe how we are doing them.

Challenge:

Observe yourself today. Notice how you speak and behave.

Observe how you feel and respond.

Observe your interactions and thoughts.

Consider:

Consider the things that:

* motivate you

* make you happy

* make you angry

* make you cry

What is it about each of these things that 'triggers' these emotions within you?

Is it a previous experience? Is it fear or anxiety?

Is it a desire to be or achieve something specific?

Watch:

Observe how you behave and respond to people when you feel:

* sad

* angry

* hurt

* content

  I suggest that you make some notes in your journal

  about your thoughts and experiences.

*   *   *

Observe the present moment:

All too often our thoughts dominate our lives. We are thinking about all the things we have to do in the future. We reflect on things that we have said and done in the past but rarely do we ponder the situation we are currently in. This time right now is called the present moment. Now is all that is real. There is no past or future, there is only right now.

If you have not already done so, I urge you to read a book called 'The Power of Now' by Eckhart Tolle. Details can be found in the bibliography. There is an audio book version available on CD.

> "As you listen to thought, you feel a conscious presence—your deeper self—behind or underneath the thought as it were. The thought then loses it power over you and quickly subsides, because you are no longer energizing the mind through identification with it. This is the beginning of the end of involuntary and compulsory thinking."
> Tolle, E (2001) Practicing The Power of Now
> (p.19)

What does it mean to be mindful?

As you are washing up, notice how the water feels? Be aware of your experience, what you can see, feel, hear and taste. Observe the bubbles popping. How do the bowls and cups look and feel? Usually while we are doing mundane chores we are talking, thinking, planning, listening to music or worse still watching the TV!

As you prepare the tea, notice the sounds that are made as the pan boils. Do these routine tasks mindfully and with an awareness of that experience.

Challenge:

Sit in 'The Now'. Be in 'The Present Moment'. This means that you will not be thinking about what you're going to make for tea or what you did yesterday. None of this matters right now. Observe your thoughts as they pass you by.

When you are doing jobs around the house, do them mindfully.

As you are eating your meal, eat mindfully.

Consider:

How did it feel to do these jobs in The Present Moment?

How did the food taste as you ate your meal mindfully?

What did you notice as you observed The Present Moment?

Watch:

Notice how your mind wonders and gently bring yourself back into The Now.

I suggest that you make some notes in your journal

about your thoughts and experiences.

*   *   *

Visualise:

Visualisation is the most powerful way to create. It's how magic is manifested. The energy is in our thoughts. I will cover the concept of manifestation shortly, but I wanted to discuss the importance of visualising first. In healing, ritual, magic and even in our daily lives, using the power of visualisation is the most essential tool in our kit. Now at this point I have to say that some people find the process of visualisation easier than others, however, I believe that it's something we can all do. For example; if I say to you "chair", what do you 'see'? We will all have an image of different things in our minds. Some people will see an actual chair (and you'd be amazed at the different varieties that are recalled), whereas, other people see the word 'chair', written in letters, others still see themselves sat down, as though in a chair, but the chair is not actually visible, the point is, we are all different, but one thing is for certain, we are all visualising and that is the key.

The meditations in this book require you to visualise to some extent. For example; protection—"seeing" a bubble of light around yourself, whereas, some people see a bubble and others just have a knowing that it's there, it's there because you've put it there and intend it to be there, so trust that it's there and so it is. Other people use the words, 'I am protected' and then know that they are, but that's still visualisation, the energy follows the thought. In fact, it's very difficult for us NOT to visualise. For instance, if I say to you 'don't think of cheese', what do you picture? Of course, it's cheese. So our intention should be to focus on what we want, rather than what we don't want and then we can create it. I will go into more detail about this when I reflect on the concept of manifestation.

In the meantime, here is a little task which I think you will enjoy, I know I did. Have a go at mapping the journey of your life so far. It's a very visual and creative activity and it can really bring insights. You might choose to make notes about your experience in your journal, although for the map itself I would urge you to use a large sheet of paper and if you need more paper, stick more sheets together with tape, rather than squashing your map to fit the page.

*   *   *

Map your Life Journey:

Life is often likened to a journey. Has your journey been an uphill climb or plain sailing?

What have been the important events in your life that have changed or affected the path you are travelling?

Who have been the key people in your life at various times?

What places, houses, buildings have been significant to you in your life so far?

Task:

Draw a map, anyway you like, showing your travels so far. Put in important landmarks such as, friends, family, homes and any major events in your life. You may like to use colours to help symbolise these events and experiences.

This map is for you. It may help you to realise where you want to be in life and the path to take from here. Use this idea to help you look more closely at your life and identify any patterns that may emerge.

You may like to show your map to a friend and talk about why you have put the things where you have. Discussing these finer points, can help you see the impact that decisions and events have on you personally, and on the outcome of your life choices.

Another map idea:

You might even like to draw a map of your future life. I would do this as a separate image. Where do you see yourself from here on in? What do you want your path to be? What life experiences do you still hope to have? Using the same approach, start to visualise life as you want it to. Start from where you are now and where you hope to end up. Focus only on what you actually want rather than any fears you may have. Bringing your attention to fears and worries just gives them energy. Bring instead to mind all that you want to have and experience and achieve in your life.

*   *   *

Energy:

Throughout this book I have referred a lot to the term 'energy'. In a way this paragraph ought to have come first, but then it would mess up my lovely 'love' acronym—so it is staying where it is, here.

Everything is energy. We are energy, all living things are energy and according to quantum physics even solid objects are energy and have their own vibrational frequency. Sometimes I find it hard to get my head around such ideas, but one thing is for certain in my life, I am well aware of energy, especial my own and other people's. Often people think about auras when I mention energy and to some extent I do mean auras, but not exclusively. Let's start with auras or the etheric body as I prefer to call it.

What is the aura?

The aura, as it is often called, is the energy body that surrounds the physical body. The first layer nearest to the physical is called the etheric body. It's often the etheric body that I am working in when giving healing—although I may touch clients physically, usually on the shoulders, head, arms, legs and feet, I mainly work on the chakras, off the body, holding my hands in the etheric body (aura) of the client.

The physical body itself is taking the healing that it needs. The energy flows through and around the physical and the energetic body. As a healer I am not *giving* the energy as such, but instead my client is *taking* the energy that they need at this time. This is why it's so important to be aware when we are giving our energy away. We may not be 'plugged into source' and this can make us feel exhausted after spending time with people who can be draining.

Cleansing the aura:

In the western world, we are very good at keeping the body clean physically. We love our bathrooms, soaps and oils, but what about our energy bodies, how do we cleanse those? I am going to suggest a couple of simple and practical ways you can ensure that your energy body is cleansed, strengthened and protected.

1. *Having an auric shower:* When having your physical wash in the shower, take the time to ground, centre and protect yourself and visualise a white light from Source also showering your body. As you're being washed and purified in the water, in your mind's eye see the light washing and purifying your etheric body.

2. *Smudging:* This is an ancient technique and one that I love and frequently use. A smudge stick is made from dried sage bound together. (Sometimes other herbs are used, but I prefer sage). The stick is lit at one end until a light smoke is emitted. Use this smoke to cleanse the energy body. Start at the top and in the aura move the stick down the energy body. You can also use it as a way to visualise the cleansing process in the same way as the shower. Work all down the front and sides (it's easier to smudge each other) and then do the back. Draw all excess or unwanted energy down and into the earth for transmutation (recycling). I also like to smudge objects, to release unwanted energy, as well as rooms, especially in the corners where energy can become stagnant. At our healing groups or whenever engaging in group meditation, we smudge each other at the start of the session. A smudge stick can be bought for a few pounds,

depending on the size you choose. I suggest keeping it in a pot or shell in case bits drop onto the floor. When lit, sometimes hot embers can drop. I put my smudge stick out in a mixture of soil, sand and grit. I have known people to put them out with water but this is a mistake as they are unable to light the stick again easily.

Healing the aura:

Often the aura needs the healing energy as much as the physical body.

I have seen clients who have had a recent shock and I have noticed that their etheric body appears as though it's been splattered. One lady I treated, her aura was in dots all around her and it wasn't like that when I'd seen her the previous week. It was like paint splats. I asked her what her week had been like and she told me about falling off her bicycle and into the road where she as nearly hit by a car. That explained it. Her aura was in shock. Thankfully healing energy can sort it out. It's this kind of situation that can occur and an inexperienced practitioner wouldn't know, or if they did have a sense of it they might not know what to do. It's the child and box of matches scenario again.

Auras can become damaged but can easily be repaired during healing. If an aura has a tear, hole, rip or is damaged then the person may lose energy and illness, emotional distress and tiredness can persist. This can be easily resolved with some simple steps. It is important that the healer scans the aura and checks for damage as part of the healing process. To give healing without doing this could be counterproductive. If there is damage then it's like running the tap with the plug out. The bath will never be filled with water. In the same way the client will not be able to continue absorbing the energy of the healing session into their physical body if they are losing it before it gets there through a damaged aura!

As I have said, energy is not only about auras. There are other energies that we need to be aware of. I could have put the word Entities into the acronym, but ultimately they are just energy too. I have heard people being dismissive about the idea that there are 'beings' which can wreak havoc on our systems. Not all of these entities are sinister or demonic; some can simply be thought-forms or fragments. Some entities can be earth-bound spirits (souls which have yet to pass over) and I've experienced a few of these in my practice. The point is that these energies vary in strength and power.

Many of the pagans I meet at conferences and events have got entity attachments in their etheric bodies or worse still inside their physical bodies. Some of these are because they have dabbled with energy they are inexperienced with, or they have actually invited these entities in as part of a ritual, or they have attended a ritual and unknowingly picked up unhelpful energy which they have continued to carry with them. There are many ways of drawing in the unwanted and I am not attempting to scare anyone, but simply, make people aware that these energies are low level and unhelpful.

If a person wishes to call upon a spirit guide or being then I always advise that they ask for the "Highest and Brightest Beings of Love, Light and Healing" or better still name the angels and ascended masters specifically. I frequently invite the angels and archangels to be with me as I channel healing, after all—it's not me doing the healing it is energy directly from Divine Source. In fact a lot of the healing work I help to facilitate is the angelic beings doing it all. I ask them and they know what to do.

As well as auras and entities there are other energetic aspects I
frequently come across which some pagans and non-pagans seem
totally unaware of. These are called Cords.

Cording and de-cording:

Whenever we have a strong connection with a person, we can be
corded to them energetically. This can be a parent-child connection
or a partner-lover connection. Usually the cords that we create
are healthy and beneficial. They are the link we have to someone.
Sometimes you may notice that you think the same things at the
same time or say something at the same time. This can be because
of your energetic connection to them. However, cords can also be
detrimental to our wellbeing if they are not healthy. They can sap
our energy or cause pain and heartache if a relationship has broken
down. When I am doing healing work on clients I always scan the
body to see if there are any unhealthy cords that are not serving
the person at this time. There is a way that you too can scan the
body to see if there are any cords that need to be cut. De-cording
from unhealthy cords is beneficial for the other person too it does
not mean that you are cutting them out of your life, you are simply
cutting away negative energy that is depleting or hindering you. This
de-cording process can often help to strengthen a relationship.

De-cording meditation:

Find a comfortable position, either lying down or sitting in a straight back chair, whichever feels best to you today. Take a few nice deep breaths, bringing your awareness fully to the present moment. Let go of any busy thoughts preventing you from tapping into your inner essence.

In your minds' eye, starting with your head, scan down your body seeing each chakra one by one and notice if there is anything that is no longer serving you. You may see cords that have withered and wilted or cords which are so thick and tough that energy can no longer freely pass through them. If you notice any cords make a mental note of them. You may like to ask who they are connected to and you might get a strong impression of a person.

When you are happy that you have identified the cords that no longer serve you, you can cut them in several ways. You can invite the angels to come along and clear them for you, this is a quick and easy process for them and they know exactly what they are doing, or you can take a crystal sword and in your minds' eye and cut the cords yourself. If you decide to do this yourself then you need to also invite the healing energy in to heal the wounds and take the debris away. Allow the white cleansing healing light to repair any wounds, holes or cords you may have, filling your body with light. Ensure that your chakras are closed to a safe and appropriate level before completion.

*   *   *

CHAPTER FIVE

Who am I?

This chapter continues the process of our personal spiritual practice using the LOVE WHO I AM acronym. We have considered—LOVE; Listen, Observe, Visualise and Energy and now we're moving onto the next group of ideas which can be used when developing our spiritual practice. WHO are your guides?

LOVE WHO I AM:

Meeting your Guides:

One of the opportunities I always appreciate having is meeting my guides. Depending on the path you have chosen, the guides, beings or animals you choose to meet will vary. The process however remains similar.

Who are these guides?

Some of them are called "beings of light" because they work within the spectrum of light and use the language of light, transmitting thought impulses into the souls of those they work with. Many high level guides are nearly pure energy, having evolved into spirit and taken on the shimmer of Divine Light. Having evolved beyond a causal plane, they work within a multidimensional reality.

Their goal is to bring insight, wisdom and awareness into our lives to enable us to achieve a higher level of consciousness. There are so many places where guides come from that it is easier to focus on the difference between the guides and be able to differentiate which guides are working for good and which are less evolved.

Entities can be from many different dimensions and realities and be at different stages in their own evolutions. It is important to be discerning about the types of guides you connect with. High level guides are primarily concerned with your spiritual growth and your safety. They are sources of guidance, clarity and direction.

How will you know?

When you meet people, you have an immediate sense of how loving and wise they are. You know if you feel good, positive and happy around them. This is the same when meeting a guide. You have the ability to recognise a guide who isn't evolved in just the same way as you have the ability to recognise wisdom in people. Truth feels as though you already know it.

What do guides do?

They come to light your path, to guide your journey through life. Their wish is for your higher good.

They help you to:

- remember who you are

- heal your wounds

- release your fears

- learn to love others

- learn to love yourself

- forgive and grow

- make choices

- use your wisdom and intuition

They support and encourage you on your journey. They give you strength and understanding.

Regardless of the path you follow or the name you give to your guides, angels, ascended masters and so on, this meditation is an opportunity for you to 'open the door' safely to meeting your spirit guides. The same meditation could be used for meeting your totem animal or animal guide.

*   *   *

Meeting your Spirit Guide Meditation

Take a moment to relax your body and as you breathe in, allow the white light to cleanse your entire being and as you exhale allow anything that no longer serves you to leave you and return to the light for transmutation.

You are about to enter your very special place, your own sanctuary. A safe place, a place you can visit at any time you choose to. As you look in front of you, there is a flight of white steps. You look at the steps, you see a soft mist coming from the side of the steps and covering each step. In a few moments I am going to invite you to take the first step, but before I do this, I want you to feel at peace and notice how tranquil and safe you are. Give yourself time before you embark on your own important journey.

Now you are ready to take your first step towards your sanctuary. On each step, you notice special objects or artifacts . . . and notice how you are feeling. You are relaxed and entering a state of deep peace and expectation. The mist is surrounding you and it makes you glow. You are ready to enter the sanctuary.

Now you are stepping through a huge archway and the mist is clearing and you can hear faint music. As you walk forward you can hear the music more clearly. The music now seems to be all around you and inside you, soft and gentle. As the mist disappears, you find yourself in a beautiful meadow. The sun is shining, the grass is emerald green and the colours around you have real depth and beauty. In front of you, there is a glistening waterfall cascading over rocks and the water runs into a clear river.

As you look up someone is coming towards you from the direction of the waterfall. You start to feel a sense of warmth and recognition. Now you are ready to meet your guide. "I would like to introduce you to your guide". Greet your guide. Notice how they look. Listen attentively to anything your guide has to say.

Your guide is your friend, guardian, and spiritual mentor. You may ask your guide any questions you wish. Now I will leave you with your guide for a few minutes, and as I do, be reminded that you can relax and enjoy what unfolds and develops in its own way, naturally. Notice what happens and trust that this is what you need at this moment.

It is now time for you to make you way back to the steps. Before you do this, listen to your guide's final words. Your guide might give you a gift or some special advice, this you should treasure. You may wish to give a gift to your guide; this can be a pledge or merely a thank you.

Now I would like you to turn into the mist and slowly return to the steps carrying your gift back into your sanctuary. You can leave your gift here or take it away with you for safe keeping. The guide that you met is your inner guide, a teacher, who helps you with any issues that trouble you. You can visit your guide whenever you need or want to and this will help you to deepen your relationship. Now begin to bring your awareness back into this room.

When you are ready, begin to open your eyes, stretch your arms, wiggle your toes and become aware of your surroundings, feeling happy and refreshed from this wonderful experience.

*   *   *

LOVE WHO I AM:

I—I (me); There are two really important points I wish to make here. Firstly, being a healer is not about the ego and ensuring that we let people know that we are channelling the healing energy is critical. Secondly, we have to take care of ourselves first. Now these comments may seem to contradict each other but I am going to expand here on what I actually mean.

The Ego:

In a therapeutic situation very often people are hurting, both physically and emotionally, they are vulnerable and they are looking for answers, for relief from their pain, for a listening ear. All too often I have seen therapists who then become popular and start displaying hugely egotistical behaviours in public situations, with comments such as "she was so ill until she came to me, I worked on her and now she's transformed" and so on. These kinds of displays are ugly and unnecessary. Please be reminded that a healer is a facilitator and a channel and that Divine Spirit (or whatever label you have chosen for Source energy) is actually doing the healing. With healing support and care humbly given, a person can essential heal themselves!

Taking care of YOU:

On the other hand, it is also essential and that YOU are taken care of. Self healing and seeing a practitioner yourself, working on your own issues and taking care of "I" is also important. Giving out to others continually and not replenishing the energy for you is also a huge mistake. You will not be any use to others if you are ill, exhausted or depleted.

On an aeroplane, we are reminded in the safety briefing that; should the cabin depressurize then oxygen masks will drop down automatically. We are told to place our own mask on first before assisting others. How can we help a small child if we are not getting the air we need ourselves? The same applies to healing. We have to work on ourselves and take care of ourselves if we want to help and support other people.

*   *   *

LOVE WHO I AM:

A—Affirmations

M—Manifestation

What are affirmations?

Using affirmations is a way to declare positive your desires. They are worded in the present tense e.g. "I am fit and healthy" not in future tenses as they may make you feel that you have to strive harder or work tirelessly to create what you want and desire in your life. Affirmations can be used in various contexts and for all sorts of reasons. Some people need them more frequently than others.

Some people have the opposite going on in their thought processes and don't even realise this. For example, do you ever think or say these types of things?

"Everything is going wrong for me today"

"I'll never make it in time"

"There's no way I am going to be able to do this"

These are examples of negative affirmations that people say to themselves without realising that what they are doing is damaging. I touched on this point previously when discussing the power of words.

Let's not focus on the negative a moment longer. I will suggest some positive affirmations here for you try out. Everyone I have ever met wants to be happy so I am offering up some happiness affirmations for you to try right now.

"I am happy"

This is a good starting point to say this even if you're not feeling it and to smile as you say it.

"I am excited about the new day and look forward to it with anticipation and interest".

"I choose to be happy at the start of each day".

"My happiness draws an overwhelming amount of blessings into my life".

"My happiness continually brings me more happiness".

So you get the idea. Affirmations can be created for all areas of your life as and when you need them. Keep them positive and keep them in the present.

Here are some affirmations for health.

"I am healthy".

"I am fit, healthy and full of vitality and energy".

"My body loves it when I eat well and exercise".

"My strong body has fully recovered and healed".

"I eat healthy, nutritious and digestible food every day".

"I take good care of myself".

Here are some general affirmations that you might like to note.

"I am at peace with my choices in life".

"I am grateful for the experiences that I have".

"My abundant thoughts and actions lead in the perfect direction of my desires".

"I am thankful for the limitless, overflowing Source of my abundance".

"I am always in the right place at the right time".

"I am a walking reflection of success and happiness".

"I create the time to spend with my friends".

When I needed affirmations I sometimes wrote them out, kept them in my pocket or bag and looked at them, read them and declared them when I needed to remind myself how truly blessed I am. This really helped me to get things into perspective. Now I have key statements in my memory that I draw upon whenever I need a boost.

How do we manifest?

We are manifesting all the time, whatever we are thinking we are creating in our lives. The point to this section is to highlight how we can *consciously create* in our lives and become people who *manifest deliberately* what we want.

The 'Law of Attraction' is a concept that states "like attracts like" energetically. Unlike magnetism which states that opposites attract. Like any universal law, it is so no matter what.

The Law of Gravity is consistent no matter how good or bad we are. If we let go of an object the universal law of gravity states that this object will fall to the ground. The same applies with the Law of Attraction. No matter what, this law is still at work, whether you choose to recognise it, believe it or deliberately create with it, it doesn't matter because the law still states that energetically "like attracts like".

What ever I think about I create. I draw to me what I am thinking, feeling and experiencing in my life. We all do. The Law of Attraction simply says that you attract into your life whatever you think about. Your dominant thoughts will find a way to manifest. So notice what you are thinking about. If I want to manifest something in my life fast then I not only think about it, I talk about it, write it down, visualise myself doing it or experiencing it and I feel the emotion associated with, For example, ask yourself, how would you feel if you desire was fulfilled? Then start feeling that emotion now. Feel the joy welling up inside you and bubbling over like a spring. This really speeds up the manifestation process. If you are a practitioner of magic and spell casting then you will already know the power of this approach, Magic is essentially the law of attraction in action. When you are spell casting you are thinking about what you want to create, you may even have it written down as a statement (affirmation) and you feel the power of it by visualising it in your mind's eye and you do a ritual, which is essentially handing over the thought/desire to the universe. Spell casting is an elaborate way of

THE HEALING POWER OF THE GODDESS; A PRACTICAL APPROACH FOR PAGANS
DEVELOPING IN THEIR SPIRITUAL PRACTICE AND THE HEALING ARTS

95

using the law of attraction. That is how magic works. As much as I can understand why people want their candles and sacred circles and ritual tools to do their magical spells, these tools are actually only a way to focus the mind and I believe quite unnecessary. I get the same results without all the paraphernalia, because I have the intention, the thoughts and the emotions which I hand over to the universe and so I create the desires in my life.

The other important point to make is that I also make sure my actions and words support my desires and thoughts when I want to create. For example, if I want to go somewhere abroad, I might think about it, visualise it and talk about it but on a practical levels I may also buy a guide book for that place and use language such as "when I go to . . . next year I will . . ."

If I want to get an interview for a job then I will organise the outfit I am going to wear for that interview, have it out ironed and ready on the hanger and start preparing for it even before the interview has been actually offered. Behaving as though it's going to be and living it now is part of that process.

In order to create this book, I thought about it, visualised it and 'saw' it on on a bookshelf and I started writing it, talking about it and behaving as though it's on its way already. As I am writing it now, the book is not yet complete, but I am thinking about the end result and the joy I will feel when I see its completed state. I am feeling that joy right now. If you're reading this, then I have fulfilled my desire and my hope to publish this book is now a reality. Your desires can be a reality too. If you are interested in finding out more about the law of attraction then take a look at the further reading suggestion at the back of this book. The most well known book and DVD is called The Secret, but I have to say that I am not a fan of the commercial way in which this book and DVD teach the law of attraction. There are more spiritual approaches to the concept of manifesting in your life and I would recommend picking up any book or audio by Jerry and Esther Hicks.

*   *   *

CHAPTER SIX

The Role of the Pagan Healer

It's not possible to write a book about developing in spiritual practice and the healing arts without also including a chapter that covers ethics and a code of practice. I have witnessed so many inappropriate circumstances and conversations at pagan events and Mind, Body, Spirit fairs and festivals. I have seen people using energy work and therapies to manipulate others. I have heard people betray confidences with idle gossip and unhelpful conversations. I have seen people frightened because a 'healer' has said something like "I sense there's something wrong here, (pointing to an area) maybe it's your liver, kidneys . . ." or whatever it is they say. It's because of these experiences and the things I have seen and heard that I am including this chapter. Some might consider it common sense, but for some reason, people still make mistakes in this vitally important area!

Confidentiality:

I am certain that you will read this sub heading and say to yourself 'well of course it goes without saying' . . . but does it . . . really? The healing world and the pagan community are small. News travels fast and people know people, even if you think they don't! If someone comes to you for spiritual support, healing or just to talk, then the number one priority has got to be confidentiality.

I have even been in group settings e.g. meditation circles, when someone has referred to a person they gave healing to (not giving a name) just to describe what happened in the session, but the details they revealed meant that I was able to identify the person they were talking about. This is totally unacceptable in my opinion. ALL circumstances should remain private. The conversations, the actual healing session and what happened, no matter how remarkable it may appear to be, confidentiality must be adhered to.

Having been a victim of disclosure myself, it is something I am very serious about in my personal practice. I do not even tell anyone who my clients are and I expect that also from the healers and therapists that I visit.

What not to say:

I am also continually surprised by the things I hear healers saying to clients in public settings. If you are working on a person, giving them healing, Reiki or doing a chakra balance and you get a sense of something, that's just it, you get a sense of something. It's not then up to you to tell your client that you sense they have got x, y or z. wrong with them. If I am in a situation where I really have a strong impression that there is in an issue then I approach this very carefully. More often than not I will say nothing. If I really feel that I need to make a comment, then it might be worded something like; "I had a really strong pulsing sensation and tingling when my hand was here". Then I see what the client says. I don't elaborate on that. If I get a throbbing in my hands then that's what I might say to the client, "I have got a real throbbing sensation when I work in this area" but I would *never* say "ooh there's something here, that's not right!" and I have heard exactly that being said to someone.

I have even heard healers commenting negatively on the prescribed medication a person is taking. This is absolutely unacceptable.

The National Federation of Spiritual Healers (NFSH) now called The Healing Trust has a clear Code of Conduct within the organisation that practitioners must adhere to. Reiki healers on the other hand have no such code of practice that is directly taught or monitored. Therefore it is up to the individual practitioner to ensure that they are maintaining a high standard in their personal practice.

Our role as healers is to put people's mind at rest, to reassure them, help them to be positive. We are *not* there to diagnose, advise on medication or make any other comments.

The Role of the Coven and Healing:

Healing is one area I know quite a few covens work with regularly and they get lots of requests for help with problems. I think it's essential that coven leaders have a full understanding of the ethics associated with their work and healing practices. I personally believe that High Priests and Priestess (regardless of their tradition) ought to be trained in the healing arts properly and have a clear understanding of the energy they are working with. Thankfully many of the ones I am familiar with do have a good foundation in these areas, but I have heard horror stories of more damage being done to people in these circumstances. I have referred to protection techniques in this book and alerted you to the dangers of entities and low levels beings. To have these safeguards in place when 'working magically' is essential on all levels. Being grounded and protected is critical especially in group settings where energy is invited into the circle.

Get to work:

Throughout the previous six chapters I have discussed what healing is and the benefits of adopting an apprenticeship approach to developing in the healing arts. I have set out techniques for plugging into source energy. I have provided guided meditation scripts for grounding, centering, protection, self-healing, distant healing, earth healing and meeting your guides. I have given examples of ways in which to develop a personal spiritual practice regularly. I have suggested the acronym LOVE WHO I AM as reminder for checking your personal spiritual development and I have reflected on the importance of an ethical approach. Now it's up to you. Take these ideas or not as you see fit. I wish you the very best with your personal life journey and healing development.

*   *   *

BIBLIOGRAPHY

Ashworth, D. (2001) Dancing with the Devil as you're Channelling the Light.

Rand, W. (1991) Reiki: The Healing Touch.

Stein, D. (1995) Essential Reiki: a complete guide to an ancient healing art.

Steine, B & F. (2005) The Reiki Sourcebook.

Tolle, E. (2001) Practicing the Power of Now.

*   *   *

FURTHER READING

Angelo, J. (1994) Your Healing Power. Piatkus Ltd, London

Angelo, J. (2002) Spiritual Healing: A Practical Guide to Hands-on Healing. Godsfield Press Ltd. UK

Hicks, J & E. (2005) Ask and it is Given: Learning to Manifest your Desires. Hay House. US

Howell, F. C. (2002) Making Magic with Gaia: practices to heal ourselves and our planet. Red Wheel. US

Huffines, L. (1995) Healing yourself with Light: How to Connect with the Angelic Healers. H. J. Kramer. Canada

Penczak, C (2004) The Witch's Shield: protection magick & psychic self-defense, Llewellyn Publications. USA

Virtue, D. (1997) the Lightworkers' Way: awakening your spiritual power to know and heal. USA

Lightning Source UK Ltd.
Milton Keynes UK
172840UK00002B/90/P